Gratitude

GINA DIAZ

BOOK SERIES BY FIG FACTOR MEDIA

WordPower Book Series

It is sold with the understanding that the publisher and the individual authors are not engaged in the rendering of psychological, legal, accounting or other professional advice. The content and views in each chapter are the sole expression and opinion of its author and not necessarily the views of Fig Factor Media, LLC.

For more information, contact:

Fig Factor Media, LLC | www.figfactormedia.com

Cover Design & Layout by Juan Pablo Ruiz
Printed in the United States of America

ISBN: 978-1-959989-37-0
Library of Congress Control Number: 2023915600

DEDICATION

I dedicate this book to my loving family.
They are what I'm most grateful for.

ACKNOWLEDGMENTS

First and foremost, I would like to acknowledge my God because, without him/her/it, I wouldn't be able to write these words or read these sentences. Thank you, God, for surrounding me with amazing people who believe in and support me.

I would like to start by thanking the one and only Jackie Camacho-Ruiz for giving me this opportunity and encouraging me daily to appreciate all the micro-moments life has to offer.

A special thanks to my supportive and ever-loving husband, Pablo Sarmiento, for sticking with me through the good, the bad, and the ugly. I am so grateful that you are my biggest supporter and cheerleader. Your positive attitude, love, and encouragement allow me to do what I love and be who I am. Thank you for loving me.

INTRO

"Thank you, God, for I am alive!" shines brightly on my phone at 7 a.m. sharp. That's how I begin each morning. Why? I'm a big believer in manifestation and setting the tone for your day—I believe the way you start your day defines the way your entire day pans out.

Gratitude is more than just saying a casual "Thank you." It's a state of mind. It's that instant, yet gentle, flutter in our hearts and stomachs brought about by the care of our loved ones. When we start our day with things that evoke that warm feeling, we are paving the way for a day filled with positivity and better experiences. These expressions of gratitude can look as simple as:

- I am grateful for opening my eyes, not everyone has that opportunity.
- I am grateful for the ability to breathe on my own, not everyone can.
- I am grateful for having a place to be every morning.
- I am grateful for having the freedom of choice.
- I am grateful I don't have to wake up next to someone I don't love.
- I am grateful for the senses I possess, including those I might not have.

Some of these affirmations may seem minor or insignificant, but that's the beauty of gratitude—it is adaptable. Even in the darkest times, expressing gratitude for the tiniest things can illuminate some aspect of our lives. Sometimes, a simple "thank you" to someone fills us with those uplifting flutters and impacts others in ways we may not even realize. Gratitude cultivates a mindset of abundance and opens doors to greater positivity in our lives.

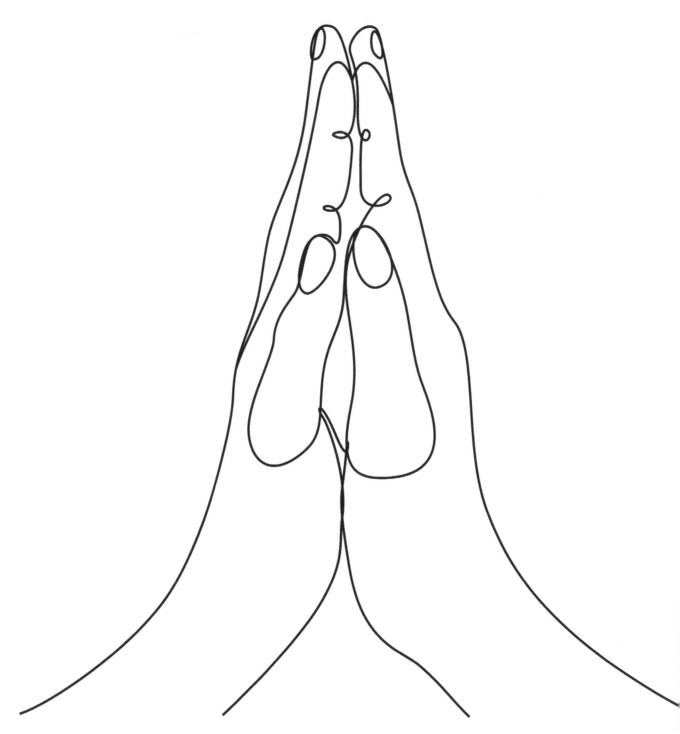

WHAT IS GRATITUDE?

Gratitude is the state of being grateful. Gratitude can have several meanings depending on the context in which it is used. But in its simplest form, it is a positive emotion that invokes a feeling of being appreciative and thankful. Gratitude is a feeling, a word, a gesture, a state of being.

Saying words such as "thank you," "much appreciated," "thanks," "be blessed," and "you are too kind," or simply smiling and showing emotion of appreciation is gratitude.

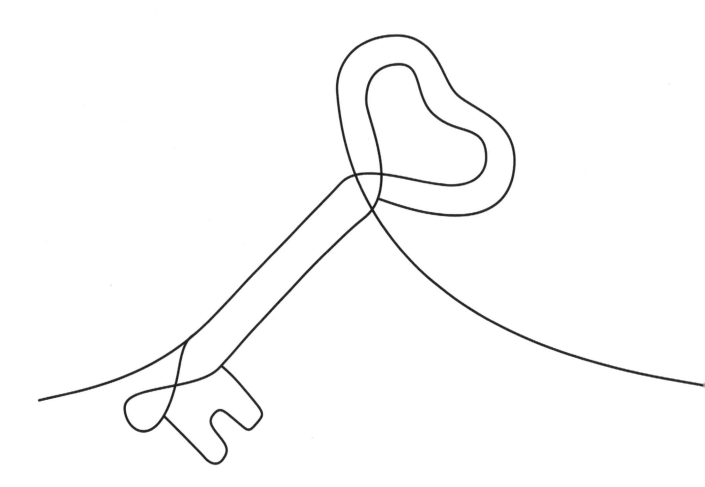

"LIVE EVERY DAY WITH AN ATTITUDE OF GRATITUDE."

– Tony Robbins

This is one of my favorite affirmations and goes back to waking up with gratitude. "Thank you, God, for I am alive today," is a great way to start your day. You see, when you start your day giving thanks, you are bound to set yourself up for a grateful day where you will be thankful for what you received/accomplished versus what you didn't get to or didn't get. Your attitude determines the type of day you will have so if you start by being grateful, how can you have a bad day?

Flip it and imagine if you start your day angry? If you start your day by talking about everything that hurts and how tired you are and how you don't want to go to work or school or wherever it is that you must go that day, you will more than likely have a negative attitude for the rest of the day.

So which one would you rather have? Gratitude is key.

BENEFITS OF GRATITUDE

Aside from setting the tone for the day, there are a lot of benefits to being grateful. Remember, after all, gratitude stems from the recognition that something great has happened to you and acknowledging that someone or something is responsible for this great thing. The practice of this can have significant POSITIVE impacts on your physical and psychological health. A few of them are:

- Better sleep
- Great self-esteem
- Less stress
- Less anxiety/depression
- Stronger and deeper relationships with others
- Confidence

All of those eventually leads to a better life and better health and all you have to do is practice the art of being grateful.

TYPES/SIGNS OF GRATITUDE

For me, waking up every day and speaking my gratitude by thanking God for waking me up is a way to get my gratitude mindset done. However, there are many ways you can practice gratitude. Expressing your appreciation and giving thanks for what you have can happen in different ways. Not everyone has to do it the same way, but it will lead to the same result as long as you say what you mean and mean what you say. Here are some examples:

- *Take a few seconds to think of one or two things in your life you are grateful for, such as:*
  - » Having a job
  - » Your kids waking up healthy and happy
  - » Your pets
  - » Maybe you or your significant other got a promotion at work

- *Stop and observe/acknowledge the beauty of something you encounter in your daily life, such as:*
  - » A tree you see every day
  - » Birds in the sky
  - » Colorful sunrises/sunsets
  - » A flower shop you pass by

- *Be THANKFUL for your health – This one is a must! For example, be thankful for:*
  - » The use of your hands
  - » The ability to use your brain and think
  - » The ability to breathe fresh air
  - » The ability to wake up and see the beauty of life
  - » Thanking someone for the positive influence they have in your life
  - » Doing something kind for another person to show you are grateful
  - » Paying attention to the small things in your life that bring you joy and peace

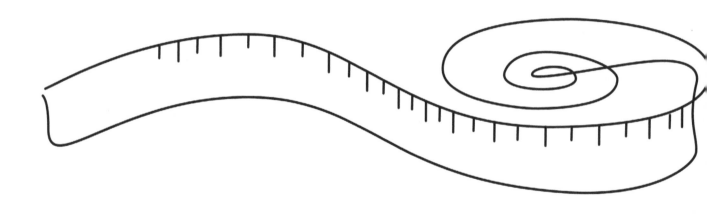

HOW DO YOU MEASURE GRATITUDE?

In my opinion, this is subjective. You—and only you—can determine this. These are a few questions you can ask yourself to measure this:

- Do you feel like you have a lot to be thankful for in life?
- Make a list: What are all the things that you have to be grateful for?
- Do you appreciate the people in your life and how do you show them this?
- Have you done enough to show people your appreciation for them or the things they do for you?
- Can you find something to be grateful for in everything you do?
- When something doesn't go your way, can you find a way to be grateful for the lesson/experience it taught you versus being upset at it not going your way?
- Are there things you could have done for others that would help them feel gratitude?
- Do you make it a habit of saying "thank you" when things are given or done for you?
- Can you name at least five things—whether it's people, things, or actions—that you are grateful for?

After answering these questions and analyzing the "YES" or "NO" and asking the "WHY" you will know how much gratitude you actually practice. Of course, more is better but don't be hard on yourself, you don't have to walk around with a smile on your face and the word thank you every minute of your life—no one does. But you should go back and analyze the good and the bad, and find the gratitude in each.

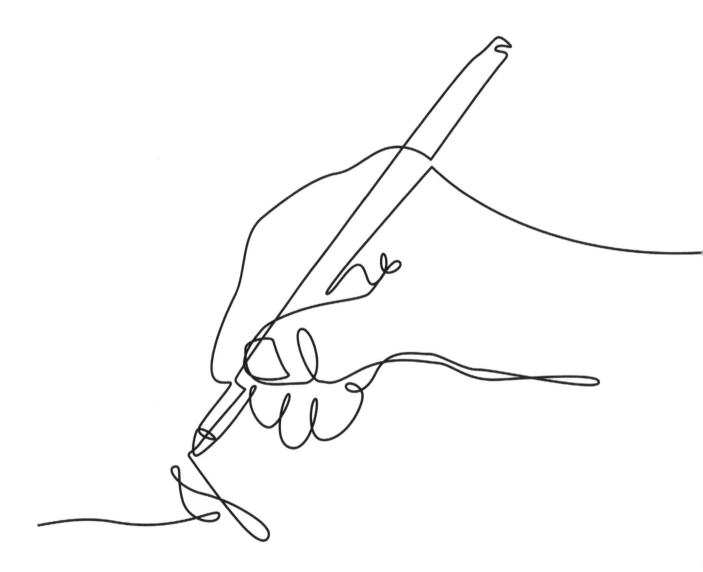

"Thankfulness is the beginning of gratitude. Gratitude is the completion of thankfulness. Thankfulness may consist merely of words. Gratitude is shown in acts."

- Henri Frederic Amiel

"Gratitude can transform common days into thanksgiving, turn routine jobs into joy, and change ordinary opportunities into blessings."

- William Arthur Ward

"Gratitude is not only the greatest of virtues but the parent of all others."

- Marcus T. Cicero

"It is not joy that makes us grateful; it is gratitude that makes us joyful."

- David Steindl- Rost

"Give thanks for a little and you will find a lot."

- Hansa Proverb

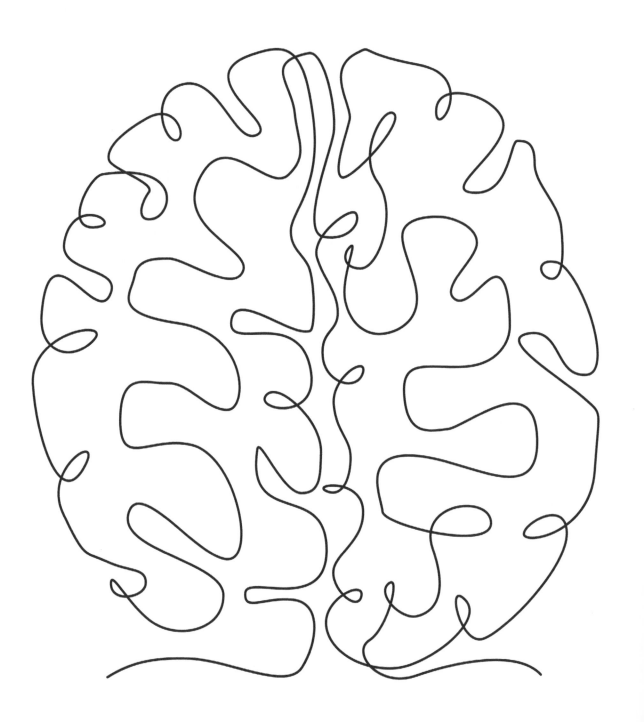

GRATITUDE AS AN EMOTION

Gratitude has multiple ways of manifesting itself. Emotion is a type of gratitude. When you have a positive feeling that inspires you to be grateful for whatever it is that inspired that feeling, that's a form of gratitude. For example, have you ever said, "God please get me through this one and I promise…" Lo and behold, God gets you through it and you have this immense feeling of relief coupled with satisfaction and you say, "Thank you God, thank you," or "I owe you one," or "Oh man, I dodged this one," accompanied with that feeling of having a big weight lifted off your shoulders? Well, that is an emotion led by gratitude.

As an attorney, I have a lot of those feelings. If I'm working on a case that may be difficult or where I just feel in my soul that I have to win this case NO MATTER WHAT, but my chances of winning are against me, I often say, "God, please help me help this person and give them a positive outcome." I sit and wait and reflect and pray, and when I get the judge's decision or the favorable letter, I get this immense feeling of accomplishment followed by relief and I cannot wait to tell my client we did the impossible. That feeling is caused by the gratitude I feel for the outcome I received. Makes sense? Think about the times you felt this, what inspired it?

GRATITUDE AS A MOOD

Sometimes people experience gratitude based on their moods. Some days you may feel more grateful than others. There may be days where you wake up so grateful that nothing can stand in the way of your grateful attitude and everything that follows is magnificent.

There may be other days, where you practice your gratitude, but it's not as prevalent as the previous day. That's all okay. As long as you have a gratitude attitude, you'll be fine.

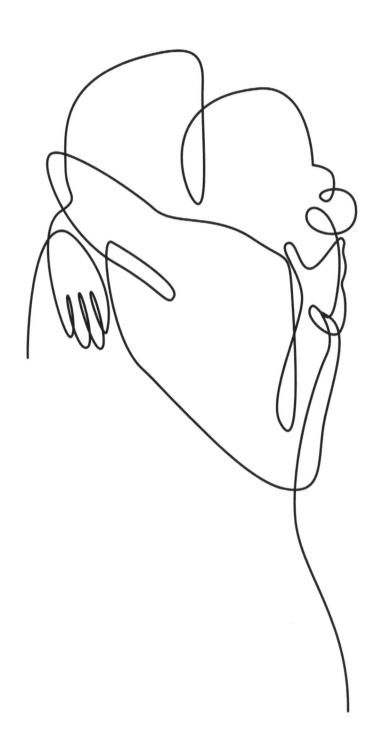

22

GRATITUDE AS AN ACTION

I am a big believer of not just saying "thank you," but showing "thank you." For example, if I have a friend who just did me a huge favor, of course I am very grateful and I will express that gratitude to her over and over again. Whenever I get the chance to show her how grateful I am, I do. It doesn't need to be anything fancy—it can be something simple as buying a nice dinner or getting something that he/she always wanted but hasn't gotten. Sometimes it may be as simple as that unexpected hug or those unexpected flowers. All of those are actions of gratitude which cause a smile and a warm feeling in the other person that is a result of my gratitude.

TIPS FOR GRATITUDE PRACTICE

Trust me, it's not easy, but it's doable. Start by simply waking up every day and saying, "Thank you for_____." Then every chance you get, whether it's when you buy your coffee or when someone opens the door for you, make sure you say, "Thank you." Pay more attention to your senses—sight, sound, taste, touch, and feel. Do they have a sense of gratitude in them you weren't aware of or is there something you are particularly grateful for?

Keep a gratitude journal and every day write something down. Then go back and reread it all the next day and add to it. Meditate and in your meditation think of all that you are grateful for to become more self-aware of the gratitude in your life.

CUP HALF-FULL OR CUP HALF-EMPTY

A few years ago, I was that person that found something wrong with almost everything I did, had, said, or liked. I would always have something negative to say and looking at my cup half-empty. I failed to see all the wonderful things I had in my life.

It all changed in 2013, when I was unexpectedly diagnosed with ovarian cancer. Luckily, it didn't spread, and after two surgeries I was fine. However, this meant that I could no longer have kids and I was left wanting to try for a boy. So, I drank my pain away, questioning why in the world this would happen to me. Looking at everything I lost, or I thought I lost. This literally continued for a year.

Until one day, I looked in the mirror and said, "Gina, aren't you tired of this? Why are you so ungrateful! You are alive!"

From that moment forward, I started giving thanks to God for being alive and for the three beautiful girls I already had. I gave thanks for being healthy despite this very serious illness. I gave thanks for all my friends and family members who prayed for me while I was sick. After this deep spiritual cleansing, I started to look at the cup half-full.

I realized that whether the cup is full or empty is based on our perception. We have more to be grateful than we realize because it is half-full 100% of the time. I concentrated on what I did have and used it to get what I needed/wanted and my cup all sudden became fuller and happier. I learned the beauty of life and appreciated every moment. Even the bad ones because they are saving you from something that you may not realize at the time.

CONCLUSION

Gratitude is one of the single most powerful feelings, emotions, and actions that one can experience in one's lifetime. Gratitude leads us to happiness, success, abundance, etc. Gratitude is the attitude. Try it and see what/how your life changes and your attitude with it, which then attracts all the great things you want/need in your life. I challenge you to try it and learn to see the fullness of your cup and you will see how the great and positive your life will become. Try it.

ABOUT THE AUTHOR

Gina Diaz, a resilient attorney, founded Diaz Case Law over a decade ago, dedicated to helping immigrants overcome challenges. With personal experience as an immigrant from Mexico, Gina understands the importance of support during tough times.

Having immigrated at five, Gina faced language barriers when starting school but conquered them through hard work. Her "I can do anything" attitude guided her through hurdles, including becoming a single mother at 19 while working at a law firm and attending college at night.

Her passion for law ignited while at a law firm, leading her to help undocumented immigrants, foreclosure cases, real estate, and businesses. Despite ovarian cancer at 33 and a business setback, Gina's resilience prevailed. She rebuilt her career while fighting for her life.

Gina, a top immigration and real estate attorney, expanded her expertise to foreclosure defense, loan modifications, and short sales. Beyond law, Gina's real estate passion led her to rehabilitate properties and co-found We Win, LLC, introducing women to real estate, and We Win, NFP, providing aid to the communities that need it the most in the chicago and surrounding suburbs.

Gina's journey showcases her determination to make a difference.

CONTACT:
IG: @abogadaginadiaz
FB: @attorneyginadiaz

HOW DOES THE WORD **GRATITUDE** EMPOWER YOU?